NUPTSE
25,726 feet

TIBET

H I M A L A Y A S

Katmandu

Mt. Everest

Thyangboche Monastery

SIKKIM

NEPAL

Darjeeling

INDIA

To Todd,
for guiding me
to Everest

Written and illustrated by
Mary Ann Fraser

On Top of the World

The Conquest of Mount Everest

Henry Holt and Company
New York

The author wishes to acknowledge the following sources: "Triumph on Everest," by Sir John Hunt and Sir Edmund Hillary, *The National Geographic*, July 1954; *The Conquest of Everest*, by Sir John Hunt, E.P. Dutton, 1953; *Tiger of the Snows*, by Tenzing Norkey, G.P. Putnam's Sons, 1955.

Published by Henry Holt and Company, Inc.,
115 West 18th Street,
New York, New York 10011.
Published simultaneously in Canada
by Fitzhenry & Whiteside Ltd.,
195 Allstate Parkway,
Markham, Ontario L3R 4T8.

Library of Congress
Cataloging-in-Publication Data
Fraser, Mary Ann.
On top of the world : the conquest of Mount Everest / written
and illustrated by Mary Ann Fraser.
Summary: Describes the final stages of the conquest of Mount
Everest on May 29, 1953, by Sir Edmund Hillary and Tenzing Norkey.
ISBN 0-8050-1578-7 (alk. paper)
1. Mountaineering –Everest, Mount (China and Nepal)—History—
Juvenile literature. 2. Everest, Mount (China and Nepal)—
Description and travel—Juvenile literature. 3. Hillary, Edmund,
Sir—Juvenile literature. 4. Mountaineers—Great Britain—
Biography—Juvenile literature. 5. Tenzing Norkey, 1914–
Biography—Juvenile literature. 6. Mountaineers—Nepal—Biography—
Juvenile literature. [1. Everest, Mount (China and Nepal)
2. Mountaineering. 3. Hillary, Edmund, Sir. 4. Tenzing Norkey,
1914– .] I. Title.
GV199.44.E85F73   1991
796.5'22—dc20   90–48988

Henry Holt books are available at special discounts
for bulk purchases for sales promotions, premiums,
fund-raising, or educational use. Special editions
or book excerpts can also be created to specification.

Printed in the United States of America
on acid-free paper. ∞

1 3 5 7 9 10 8 6 4 2

*I*t was May 28th, 1953. With feelings of loneliness and excitement, Edmund Hillary and Tenzing Norgay watched the last of their companions head down the mountain. It had taken eight months, an army of men, and three tons of supplies to get them to where they now stood, 1,100 feet from the summit. In the morning they hoped to be the first ever to climb the highest mountain in the world—Mount Everest.

As their companions faded from view, Hillary and Tenzing began preparations for the night. Already they had climbed many miles from Katmandu, the expedition's starting point. But over the next twenty-four hours would come their greatest obstacles.

Straddling the border between Tibet and Nepal, Everest rises 29,028 feet out of the world's youngest—and highest—mountain range, the Himalayas. Near the top of the world, the air has only one third the oxygen found at sea level. Breathing the thin air, climbers can suffer physically and mentally. But the weight of oxygen tanks and frames also makes climbing more difficult.

Hillary counted their remaining oxygen canisters. They had fewer than they had hoped for. But the men knew that if they were ever to make it to the top, this was their best chance. In winter, the fierce winds called monsoons that scoured Everest's sides would defeat the best of climbers. Summer monsoons brought heavy snows that increased the risk of an avalanche or a fatal slip. Only during a few days in late spring and early autumn was Everest climbable at all. But even in May, the weather could change at any moment and crush all hopes of success.

For four hours Hillary and Tenzing scraped the frozen ground to make a platform and pitch their cotton-and-nylon tent. At five miles above sea level, it was the highest anyone had ever camped.

Both men were experienced mountaineers. Edmund Hillary, a beekeeper from New Zealand, had proven his mountain-climbing skills in the Himalayas in 1951 and 1952. This was his first attempt at Mount Everest.

Tenzing Norgay, a Sherpa born in Nepal, had spent most of his life in Everest's shadow. The Sherpas are a people who came to eastern Nepal from Tibet. They call the mountain Chomolungma, which means "Mother Goddess of the Earth." Because they are adapted to the high altitude and extreme weather of their home-land, Sherpas are born mountaineers.

But no one had seen more of the world's highest mountain than Tenzing. He had first explored Everest as a porter in 1935, and had been a member of five more expeditions. For this reason Colonel John Hunt, head of the 1953 British attempt, had asked Tenzing to be his guide and *sirdar*, or leader of the Sherpas hired to assist the expedition.

After a dinner of canned apricots, dates, and sardines, Hillary and Tenzing drifted into restless sleep.

All night long icy gusts of wind tried to snatch their tent from its ledge. But the gods of Chomolungma were with them. By four in the morning, when they crawled from their sleeping bags, it was calm. The thermometer read –27 degrees Fahrenheit.

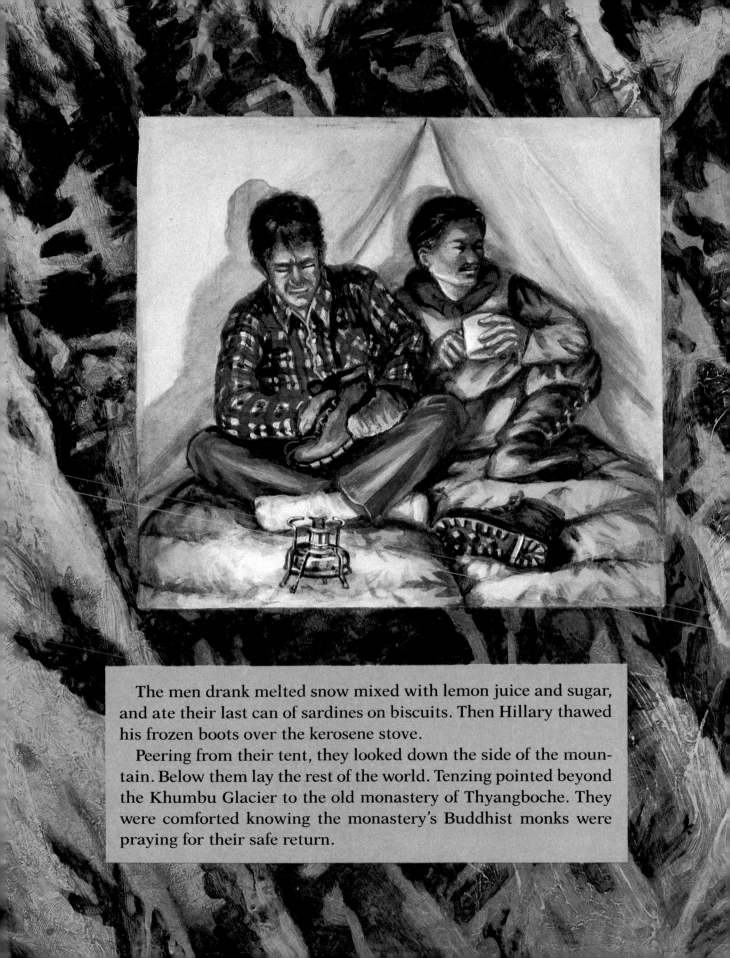

The men drank melted snow mixed with lemon juice and sugar, and ate their last can of sardines on biscuits. Then Hillary thawed his frozen boots over the kerosene stove.

Peering from their tent, they looked down the side of the mountain. Below them lay the rest of the world. Tenzing pointed beyond the Khumbu Glacier to the old monastery of Thyangboche. They were comforted knowing the monastery's Buddhist monks were praying for their safe return.

At 6:30 A.M. Tenzing and Hillary strapped on their thirty-pound oxygen packs. They knew that without them they could die. They would have only four and a half hours to reach the top and return before their oxygen ran out.

Linked by a nylon rope, they began their final ascent. Each wore a down suit protected by another windproof layer of clothing, three pairs of gloves, a hat, and snow goggles. To help them climb, they had strapped steel spikes called crampons to the soles of their boots. Each boot had an inner waterproof lining and inch-thick insulation, and weighed over two pounds.

Hillary and Tenzing were not the first to attempt to reach the summit. The first expedition was in 1922, a year after Tibet opened its borders to foreigners. Eight times since then, the monstrous peak had sent the world's best mountaineers back in defeat. It had taken the lives of at least thirteen men. Each time, the effects of extreme cold, altitude, and terrain had won. Only the year before, Tenzing and Swiss mountaineer and guide Raymond Lambert had been just a thousand feet from the summit when fierce winds and cold turned them back.

But on the clear, frosty morning of May 29th, Tenzing and Hillary had the strongest start yet. From the start of the 1953 expedition, all fifty-three members had worked to advance supplies from camp to camp up the mountain. They knew that the higher the final camp was, the more likely the men would reach the summit before their oxygen ran out.

Colonel John Hunt had decided to send Tom Bourdillon, an excellent rock climber, and Charles Evans, an experienced mountaineer, to try for the summit first. On May 23, this First Team left for Camp VIII, at the South Col. In the meantime, the remaining men moved supplies farther up the mountain. If the First Team failed, Tenzing and Hillary would try for the top from an even higher location.

Three days later Bourdillon and Evans stumbled back to the South Col, where the others were waiting. They had run out of oxygen, energy, and time three hundred feet from the top of Everest.

The next day the Second Team was moved into position, at Camp IX. It was now up to them alone to climb the last 1,100 feet.

Steadily they kicked steps in the snow, breathing from the oxygen canisters secured to their backs. The strain of each movement prevented them from speaking, yet they worked together as a team.

About four hundred feet from the South Peak's face, the men came to an abrupt stop. Which way should they go? Bourdillon and Evans had taken the ridge, but its loose snow made it dangerous. Hillary and Tenzing decided to take the face route. Cautiously they chipped steps straight up the mountainside, knowing that if they zigzagged, the undercut snow could avalanche.

They were halfway up Everest's treacherous
Southeast Ridge when suddenly the powdery
snow broke away. Hillary slid several feet before
he could stop his fall with his ice ax.

"I don't like this," he gasped. "Shall we go on?"

Tenzing replied, "Just as you wish."

They knew the risks were great, but the goal was worth it. This was not a competition to see who could reach the top of the world first. It was more like a relay race, with each expedition, each man, passing on new gains in experience and knowledge to the next. Now it was Tenzing and Hillary's turn to carry on the work of all who had tried before.

Carefully they pushed on.

Finally, at 9 A.M., they reached the 28,700-foot South Peak. No one had ever gone higher.

After a brief rest to check their oxygen supply and study the ridge ahead, they continued their dangerous climb. To their relief the snow was firm.

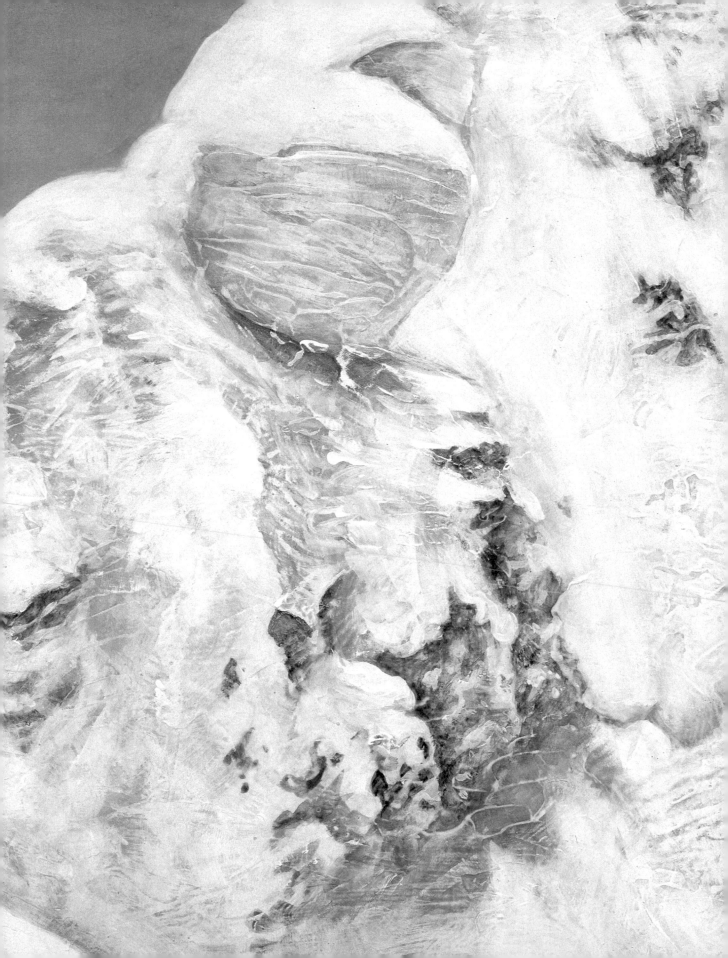

Their axes rang out in unison as they chopped steps up the razor-like ridge. They had to be more careful than ever now. To their right, great overhanging cornices of snow stuck out like twisted fingers above a 10,000-foot drop. To their left were plunging cliffs of windswept rock.

They could see the tents of Camp IV more than a mile below. Like a giant bird Hillary flapped his arms, but he knew he was too far away for the men at the camp to see him.

As they continued on, step by icy step, Tenzing began fumbling with his oxygen equipment. Hillary stopped, and discovered that ice had completely blocked the tube through which Tenzing was exhaling. Quickly Hillary cleared it so his partner could get fresh oxygen again. He then checked his own equipment and cleaned out the ice from the exhaust tubes.

But with one danger averted, they found themselves staring at an even greater barrier: A giant rock, forty feet high, blocked the ridge. There seemed to be no way over it and no way around it. Had Everest won again?

Then they noticed a small crack that rose like a chimney between the rock and cornice of ice. Hillary wedged himself into the chimney. Pushing with each part of his body and kicking with his boots, he slowly wriggled his way upward. At any moment the cornice could split away. His only safety lay in the rope Tenzing had wrapped around his ax and driven into the snow.

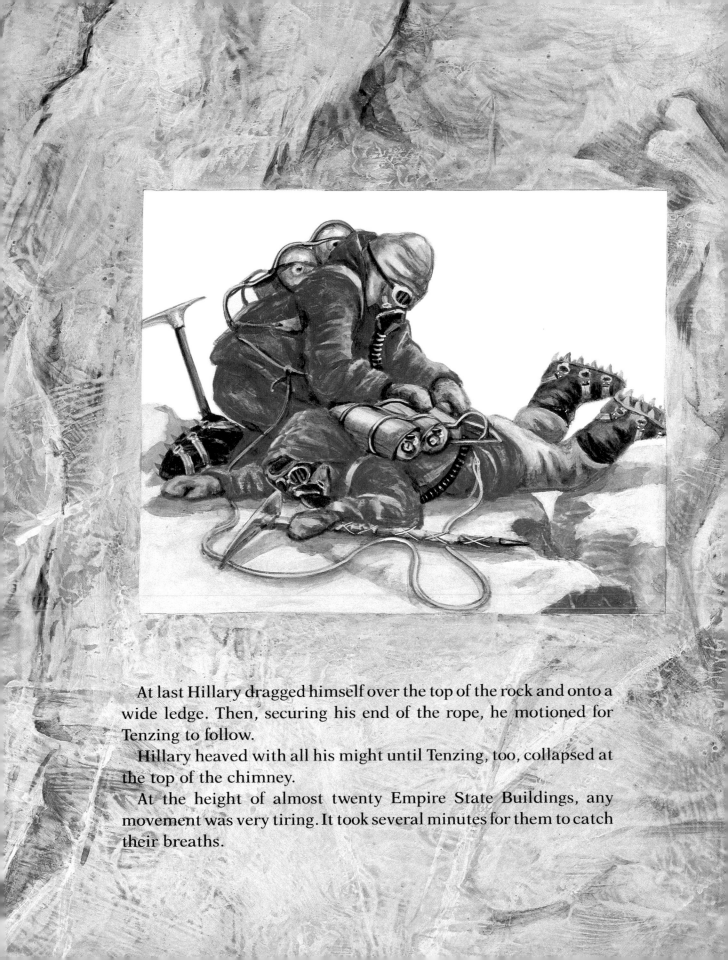

At last Hillary dragged himself over the top of the rock and onto a wide ledge. Then, securing his end of the rope, he motioned for Tenzing to follow.

Hillary heaved with all his might until Tenzing, too, collapsed at the top of the chimney.

At the height of almost twenty Empire State Buildings, any movement was very tiring. It took several minutes for them to catch their breaths.

Ahead, the ridge rolled in a series of seemingly never-ending humps. As the men climbed over one, another always loomed ahead. Their boots felt like lead, and their packs grew heavier with each step. Time was quickly passing, and there was still no sign of the summit. With each bite of the ax, shards of ice and rock were hurled into the air.

It was now 11:30 A.M. Their oxygen supply was dwindling, and in a few minutes they would have to turn back defeated.

Once more Hillary looked ahead, and suddenly realized the ridge didn't rise up, but fell sharply away. With a glimmer of hope the two climbers whacked more steps in the firm snow.

Beyond them lay a dome of ice. It stood like an island surrounded by an ocean of snow-capped peaks. The summit. But was it safe? Could it break away?

Probing with their axes, they cautiously staggered the last few yards. At last they stood on the highest point on earth, 29,028 feet above the sea. From the top of the world, they could see four countries: Tibet to the north, Sikkim to the east, India to the south, and Nepal to the south and west.

The moment was too great for words. Tenzing threw his arms around Hillary and thumped him on the back.

Then Tenzing unwound from his ax a string of flags: one for the United Nations, one for Britain, one for Nepal, and one for India. Hillary turned off his oxygen and removed his mask. Then he pulled out the camera he had kept warm beneath his shirt and took some pictures. These would be proof that they had made it. They were on top of the world!

A Final Note

Hillary and Tenzing spent only fifteen minutes on Everest's peak because of their limited oxygen supply. But before their return to camp, they left gifts of thanks to the Buddhist gods the Sherpas believe live on Chomolungma. Buried on top of the world are a small blue pencil that belonged to Tenzing's daughter, biscuits, lollipops, a chocolate bar, and a cross from Colonel Hunt.

When Hillary and Tenzing reached Camp VIII, their friends rushed out to greet them with oxygen, hot drinks, and shouts of "Everest has had it!" It was a victory for all the members of the mountaineering party.

But why was this expedition successful when all others had failed? One reason was that climbers from the eleven previous Everest expeditions had willingly shared their experience and knowledge.

Access to Mt. Everest was first allowed in 1921 by the government of Tibet. Two of the most famous early climbers were George Leigh-Mallory and Andrew Irvine, who in 1924 vanished along the Northeast Ridge. No one knows how high they were able to climb before they died. It was Mallory who, when asked why he wanted to climb Mt. Everest, replied, "Because it is there."

Bad weather, avalanches, and lack of oxygen turned back the expeditions that followed. Southern access to the peak was made possible in 1949, when Nepal opened its borders to foreigners. The most helpful of the later expeditions was made by the Swiss. It was on their climb in 1952 that Tenzing and Raymond Lambert came within a thousand feet of the summit.

Another reason for Hillary and Tenzing's success was the superior planning by Colonel Hunt, the expedition's leader.

When selecting climbers, he looked for men between the ages of twenty-five and forty with experience scaling the Himalayas and the ability to work selflessly with others. Fourteen men were chosen, including Michael Ward, who was to be the doctor. It was his responsibility to help prevent the illnesses that had plagued earlier expeditions. In addition, thirty-eight Sherpas were hired to carry supplies up the mountain.

Colonel Hunt had the men make practice climbs in Wales, the Alps, and the Himalayas. These treks enabled them to come together as a team and test new equipment and rations.

Superior supplies also gave the 1953 expedition an advantage over earlier teams. Improvements included tents made of a new cotton-nylon weave, two new styles of boots designed to prevent frostbite, and sleeping bags with both an inner and outer layer of down.

The use of more efficient and reliable oxygen sets, both closed circuit and open circuit, was the greatest improvement of all. Hillary and Tenzing used the open circuit, which mixed oxygen with the outside air. The closed circuit, used by Evans and Bourdillon, fed pure oxygen through a bag. The new systems allowed the climbers to conserve energy and climb faster, with less risk of depleting their oxygen supply.

Many countries have since sent people to Mt. Everest's summit, using further technological advancements. In 1963, Americans made the first traverse of the mountain, and six men reached the summit. Twenty-five years later, the Japanese made the first television broadcast from the top. In 1989, the first two women, both Americans, reached the peak. And in 1990, Sir Edmund Hillary's son, Peter, followed in his father's footsteps to stand on the world's highest point.

The conquest of Mt. Everest was the ultimate mountaineering test for Hillary and Tenzing. But it was also the fulfillment of a dream for those who had tried before, and an inspiration for all mountain adventurers to follow.

Glossary

altitude: the height of an object above sea level

avalanche: the sudden movement of a large mass of snow, ice, or rock down a mountainside

Buddhist: a member of the Eastern religion that grew out of the teachings of Gautama Buddha

canister: a can or tank used to hold compressed gas

chimney: a narrow crack rising up through rock or ice

col: a depression, or pass, in a mountain chain

cornice: a mass of snow or ice overhanging a ridge, usually formed by the wind

cwm (pronounced "coom"): an enclosed valley on the side of a mountain or hill

down: stuffing made from soft, fluffy goose or duck feathers

glacier: a large mass of ice that moves slowly down a slope

icefall: the broken blocks of ice created when a glacier moves down a steep slope

monsoon: a South Asian wind that blows southwest in summer (the wet monsoon) and northeast in winter (the dry monsoon)

porter: one who carries supplies

Sherpa: a member of a people originally from Tibet who live on the high eastern slopes of the Himalayas in Nepal

sirdar: a Hindi word for a person holding a high position of responsibility; the leader of the Sherpas on a mountaineering expedition

terrain: the physical features of an area of land

Thyangboche Monastery: a center for the Buddhist religion in Nepal

traverse: to cross the slope of a mountain